Culture & Leisure Services
Red Doles Lane
Huddersfield, West Yorks HD2 1YF

This book should be returned on or before the latest date stamped below. *Fines are charged if the item is late.*

You may renew this loan for a further period by phone, letter, personal visit or at www.kirklees.gov.uk/libraries, provided that the book is not required by another reader.

NO MORE THAN THREE RENEWALS ARE PERMITTED

Raintree is an imprint of Capstone Global Library Limited, a company incorporated in England and Wales having its registered office at 7 Pilgrim Street, London, EC4V 6LB
Registered company number: 6695582

www.raintreepublishers.co.uk
myorders@raintreepublishers.co.uk

Text © Capstone Global Library Limited 2014
First published in hardback in 2014
Paperback edition first published in 2015
The moral rights of the proprietor have been asserted.

Edited by Abby Colich, Dan Nunn, and Catherine Veitch
Designed by Marcus Bell
Picture research by Tracy Cummins
Production by Victoria Fitzgerald
Originated by Capstone Global Library Ltd
Printed and bound in China

ISBN 978 1 4062 6336 7 (hardback)
17 16 15 14 13
10 9 8 7 6 5 4 3 2 1

ISBN 978 1 4062 6344 2 (paperback)
18 17 16 15 14
10 9 8 7 6 5 4 3 2 1

British Library Cataloguing in Publication Data
Colich, Abby.
Rubber. – (Exploring materials)
620.1'94-dc23
A full catalogue record for this book is available from the British Library.

Acknowledgements
We would like to thank the following for permission to reproduce photographs: Getty Images pp. 4 (© Tuan Tran), 7 (© Jay P. Morgan), 9 (© Goh Seng Chong/Bloomberg); Shutterstock pp. 5 (© Vitaly Titov & Maria Sidelnikova), 6a (© Cheryl Casey), 6b (© Marie C Fields), 6c (© fred Goldstein), 6d (© daniaphoto), 8 (© Anatoli Styf), 10, 23b (© Blazej Lyjak), 11 (© Vladimir Melnik), 12 (© stoykovic), 13 (© ArtmannWitte), 15 (© Olegusk), 16 (© Jeannette Meier Kamer), 17 (© AISPIX by Image Source), 18 (© Diego Cervo), 19 (© Maridav), 21 (© Blend Images), 22 (© S.A.S Photography, © Neale Cousland, © Vitaly Korovin), 23a (© Maridav); Superstock pp. 14 (© Juice Images), 20 (© Image Source).

Front cover photograph of a girl on a tyre swing reproduced with permission of Getty Images (© LWA/Dann Tardiff).

Back cover photograph reproduced with permission of Shutterstock (© Vladimir Melnik).

We would like to thank Valarie Akerson, Nancy Harris, Dee Reid, and Diana Bentley for their assistance in the preparation of this book.

Contents

What is rubber?

Rubber is a material.

Materials are what things are made from.

Many things are made from rubber.

Rubber has many different uses.

Where does rubber come from?

rubber

Some rubber comes from trees.

Some rubber is made by people.

Rubber can be recycled or reused.

Recycled rubber can be used to make new things.

What is rubber like?

Rubber can be soft.

Rubber can be hard.

Rubber can bounce.

Rubber can stretch.

How do we use rubber?

Tyres are made of rubber.

Some toys are made of rubber.

Rubber gloves protect our hands.

Rubber boots protect our feet.

rubber

We use rubber at school.

swimming cap

We use rubber when we exercise.

Quiz

a

b

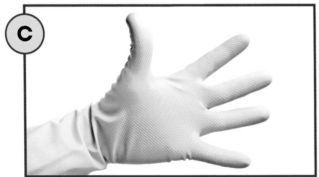

c

Which of these things are made of rubber?

Answer on page 24.

Picture glossary

protect keep safe. Rubber boots keep feet safe from getting wet.

recycle make used items into new things

Index

The **flip-flops (a)** and **glove (c)** are made of rubber.

Notes for parents and teachers
Before reading
Ask children if they have heard the term "material" and what they think it means. Reinforce the concept of materials. Explain that all objects are made from different materials. A material is something that takes up space and can be used to make other things. Ask children to give examples of different materials. These may include glass, plastic, and rubber.

To get children interested in the topic, ask if they know what rubber is. Identify any misconceptions they may have. Ask them to think about whether their ideas might change as the book is read.

After reading
- Check to see if any of the identified misconceptions have changed.
- Show the children examples of rubber, including rubber bands, erasers, and a rubber toy.
- Pass the rubber objects round the children. Ask them to describe the properties of each object. Is the object heavy or light? Does it bounce or stretch? What are the colours? Ask them to name other items made from rubber.